TO JONA

†

DONALD

1 MAY 2018

UNKNOWN WARRIOR
the war of tommy atkins

UNKNOWN WARRIOR
the war of tommy atkins

Poetry by
Donald Cooper

Drawings by
Graham Watson

ARTHUR H. STOCKWELL LTD
Torrs Park, Ilfracombe, Devon, EX34 8BA
Established 1898
www.ahstockwell.co.uk

British Library Cataloguing-in-Publication Data.
A catalogue record for this book is available
from the British Library.

ISBN 978-0-7223-4501-6
Printed in Great Britain by
Arthur H. Stockwell Ltd
Torrs Park   Ilfracombe
Devon EX34 8BA

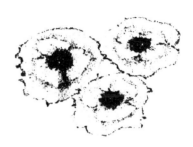

In memory of my dear brothers Douglas (Doug) and Anthony (Tony) who fought the good fight but lost their battle with cancer and also my youngest brother Alan (Flogger)

'Tommy Atkins'

It is not certain when the name 'Tommy Atkins' was first used by the British Army but it is thought to have been in use before the start of the First World War. One authority attributes its beginning to that of a British soldier, named Tommy Atkins, who served in the 33rd Foot Regiment under the command of the Duke of Wellington. Tommy described by the Duke as a 'giant of a man', was killed during hand to hand fighting in Flanders in 1794. He could neither read, nor write, and the Duke related that as Tommy Atkins lay dying his final words to the Duke were "It's alright Sir, it's all in a day's work". In 1815 the Duke of Wellington was asked to suggest a collective name for British soldiers and chose the appellation 'Tommy Atkins' in memory of this fine soldier. He justified his choice by saying that 'Tommy Atkins' embodied the key strengths of the British Army soldier.

At a later date the name 'Tommy Atkins' was used by the British Military authorities during the preparation of a new pocket ledger, ordered to be carried by each soldier. The ledger, which contained a soldier's name, age etc. quickly became known as the 'Tommy Booklet' and its holder, inevitably, as a 'Tommy'.

The idea that the name 'Tommy' preceded the start of World War One is supported by reports that German soldiers would toss pieces of paper into the British lines addressed to 'Tommy', or shout "Hey Tommy". (The trench lines separating both the

British/French and the Germans were sometimes only a matter of a few feet apart.)

The fact that an eighteenth century 'Tommy Atkins' conceivably lies buried in the Flanders soil alongside a twentieth century 'Tommy Atkins' I find intriguing.

Donald Cooper

In this poetry book 'Tommy Atkins' joins the British Army, in 1914, as a seventeen year old, as many young men of his time did. He dies during the Third Battle of Ypres, in 1917, at the age of twenty.

'Tommy' wears many different cap badges, in remembrance of the thousands that fought and fell during the Great War, as he takes his imaginary journey through the Ypres Salient, the Somme and Passchendaele battlefields.

The events, depicted after his death, are also imaginary, but I like to feel there is a spiritual truth behind them.

For the Fallen

They went with songs to battle; they were young,
Straight of limb, true of eye, steady and aglow.
They were staunch to the end against odds uncounted,
They fell with their faces to the foe.

'They shall grow not old, as we that are left grow old;
Age shall not weary them, nor the years condemn.
At the going down of the sun and in the morning
We shall remember them'

They mingle not with their laughing comrades again;
They sit no more at familiar tables at home;
They have no lot in our labour for the day-time;
They sleep beyond England's foam.

Laurence Binyon

'For the Fallen' was first published in
The Times on 21 September 1914

Contents

Part One

Recruitment Office – August 1914

"Can I join the army, Sir?"
"You can't" I heard with sorrow,
"Because you're only sixteen years,
But try again, tomorrow,
Don't tell me then you're not eighteen,
Just sign – your life I'll borrow";
"I'm back just like you said I could,
My life is yours to borrow",
"Well thank you, son", the Sergeant said,
Without a hint of sorrow;
So I signed to keep my promise,
On the form he gave to me,
And boldly printed underneath,
My new name 'Atkins Thomas'

Back Home

"I'm home Mum, I've signed on Mum –
don't cry Mum, all my mates are going,
Tell her Sis, I'll be alright –
my country needs me Mum,
I'll be back home by Christmas,
Well that's what Kitchener said!"

(The Western Front – September 1914)

Marching Soldiers

So, off I went through fields still sodden,
With blood of men too soon forgotten;
Tunic torn and heels downtrodden,
Marching proud to war;

Digging trenches and latrines,
Topped with sandbagged canvas screens,
Mess tins filled with spuds and beans,
For men who marched to war;

Cries I heard across the lines,
As men lay bleeding, making signs,
But I just turned in strange decline
from men who fell in war;

Early morning pallid shafts of light,
Played on khaki corpses of the night,
On 'Tommies' who had lost the fight
and marched no more to war.

In those few weeks Tommy learnt too well,
The meaning of a fight, the terror and the hell;
What seemed such fun turned into mud and gore,
And in his heart he felt the pity of a war.

(October 14 – November 22 1914)

First Battle for Flanders (Ypres)

Nine and thirty pointless days, over five weeks long,
Sixty thousand dead and wounded, what went wrong?
I've seen graves filled with whole and shattered bodies,
Covered with soil, and marked with wooden pins.

Name on name sent back to 'Blighty',
Names like mine, like poor old Tommy Atkins;

The Gaps are filled with new recruitment,
Though their shells and bombs are spent,
We have to stay and face the Germans,
We have to hold this salient;

Form on form sent back to 'Blighty',
Forms for ammo, just for Tommy Atkins;

The French, I'm told, are sick of fighting,
Along their lines too many men have died,
They sit with fists of whitened knuckle
at the whizzing of the shells,
Their legs inclined to bend or buckle,
As their chums are sent to heaven, via hell.

(24 December 1914)

Silent Night

Through the darkness snowflakes fell,
Thick and fast upon the trench,
As minds re-lived the horrors of the fight;
Then a German voice came singing,
Through the cold and silent air,
And the words he sang 'Oh Holy, Silent Night';

First we smiled and then we wondered
if our ears were hearing right,
As we peered across the soft and fallen white,
Then our smiles turned into laughter,
For we saw a German soldier there,
And we sang the hymn together 'Silent Night';

Christmas trees were brightly shining,
As we heard the soldiers sing
'All is calm and all is bright'
So we stood and hugged each other,
Praying hard for concord here,
On that very special Holy Christmas night.

Trench Talk with Cpl 'Jock' McCabe

I always will remember, Jock, that crazy Christmas time,
When 'Silent Night' was carolled, Jock, upon a midnight chime,
And for a while we rested, Jock, amid the mud and grime,
Thinking of our loved ones, Jock, as we sang that Christmas rhyme.

(25 December 1914)

Christmas Day Burials

Day by day, those winter days,
Bore witness to the dying, where they lay
amongst the mutilated dead,
Men, soft crying, whimpering in miserable pain,
Men, hard dying, hoping help might come,
Before the Angel of Death came visiting
but dying all the same,
Those soldiers who would have their names
inscribed on cross or 'missing' wall,
Long after that Christmas Day;

Day by day the many died,
Week by week they did abide
in attitude of death and grotesque shape;
Through the late months of that year,
Men lay rotting in no man's land,
Decaying in the rain and winter snow,
That was the anguish of their deaths,
and not the glory of their deeds,
Side by side those fallen warriors remained,
Waiting for an act of human consideration,
On those days before that Christmas Day.

And so they met upon that Christmas Day,
Agreeing that, before the evening darkness held its sway,
They would redeem the dead, whose needs were basic now,
Rescue them from their seemingly futile sacrifice,
Khaki and grey alike – round helmet or Prussian spike,
Their comrades would be laid to rest,
By comrades who would do their best
to cover them, with earth and Christian dignity,
Upon that special Christmas Day.

The Christmas truce (German: *Weihnachtsfrieden*, French: *Trêve de Noël*) was a series of widespread, unofficial ceasefires, which took place along the Western Front around Christmas 1914, during World War One. Through the week leading up to Christmas, parties of German and British soldiers began to exchange seasonal greetings and songs between the trenches; on occasion, the tension was reduced to the point that individuals would walk across to talk to their opposite numbers bearing gifts. As well as joint burial ceremonies, several meetings ended in carol-singing. Troops from both sides were friendly enough to play games of football with one another. Source: Wikipedia

(26 December 1914)

Christmas Football Match

Two o'clock in the morning, the frost lying deep,
Tommy Atkins trying hard to get some sleep,
Flexing aching thighs and stiffening calf muscles,
Did yesterday really happen,
Were we actually happy and keen,
Or have I just woken from a wishful dream?
Can it really be right, during yesterday's light
we played football against the 'detestable' Hun,
In a match that the enemy won;

Three goals to two the score,
But unlike the goddamn on-going war,
Nothing was lost but our pride,
Dozens of 'Tommies' and Germans,
Formed spirited national teams
and chased 'tatty' football, scratch covered, but round,
Over cleared yards of snow covered ground,
Which earlier served as a land of no man,
Except for the dead of this war

In a period of continuation, between waking and sleep,
Tommy's mind drifted back to the sight
that he witnessed, and joined in, with schoolboy delight,
Where football and sport held its breath-taking sway,
On that festive and beautiful great Christmas Day;
As his aching and shaking muscles relaxed,
Tommy slept through the peace of a heaven sent night,
That followed a magical day.

Field Service
Post Card

1p

Mrs M Atkins

33 The Avenue

Wakeford

County Anywhere

England

UK

Dear Mum
I got your card today and, yes, I'm feeling great,
Although some days I get confused about the time and date,
The foods OK although it's true I am a wee bit slimmer,
Saturday I saw Sir Haig, well just a little glimmer,
Can't pronounce the town I'm in, the lads all call it 'Wipers'
Two of our young Officers got shot at by a sniper;
By the way, how are twins and are they walking yet,
And how is Ben, my Labrador, since you took him to the vet?
Love to Sis and Auntie Peg, the weather here is awful,
Hope to be on leave quite soon

Your son (now Acting Corporal)

(Ypres Salient – April 1915)

Behind the German Lines

Have you seen the sight they make?
those shining bayonets,
Pointing from their sandbagged holes,
Making flashing threats;
We hate the 'Dinks',
Those 'Aussie sports'
The 'Taffys' are, we think,
As stubborn as a mule;
We badly need more fuel,
Rifles and small arms ammunition.

Crash bang hell, 'Tommy's in his well,
The trench we filled with water,
Whilst waiting for the slaughter;
Drink your rum, console your chum
But save a drop for me!

'O' to be in Strasbourg now the spring is there,
'O' to be in Munich, drinking all that beer,
'O' to be in England, with no war to fear,
'O' to be victorious, singing songs of cheer.

Have you heard the sounds they make?
Those bloody 'Mills' grenades?
They're not supposed to fight like us,
Those tiresome 'Brit' Brigades;
We hate the French,
Our bunkers stench,
And fear the Sappers' tunnels;
Please God the ridge won't blow;
Our rations are too low.

Crash bang, swell, 'Tommy's not too well
still knee deep in water,
Waiting for the slaughter;
Kneel in prayer, protest you're there,
But say a prayer for us!

'O' to be in Paris, sailing down the Seine,
'O' to be in Holland, without the blooming rain,
'O' to be surrounded by good food and wine,
'O' to be on Furlough, where everything is fine.

Ypres Salient – April 1915

Behind the British Lines

Rise up men, rise up then,
And sing this song with me,
Rise up men, collect again,
Your bombs and ammunition,

There was 'Jerry' on the ridge,
With us 'Tommies' on the bridge,
But the water was a flood,
Coloured red with all our blood;
And our faces were all pale,
In this hell called Passchendaele;

I wonder what the heck it's like,
Out on those numbered hills,
Are the 'Boche' as petrified,
I wonder how they feel?
Can't they hear us digging
in the chalk beneath their feet?
Sometimes I just wonder if it's real.

(Ypres Salient – April 1915)

The Death of Hill Sixty

Then we blew that hill to bits, poor old number sixty,
Yes, the Sappers dug it well, poor old number sixty,
Sixty-two, and more, along the line;
And the blast was heard in England,
With an echo on the Rhine;
But they still did not give way,
So we fought the Hun all day;

There's still 'Jerry' on the ridge, lots of 'Tommies' on the bridge,
And the waters now a flood, coloured red with German blood,
As the wounded tell their tales,
In this place called Passchendaele.

Trench Talk with Capt. Watkins

This fighting and this killing, Sir, chill me to the bone
Don't know what else to say, Sir, you've heard it all before,
Didn't think it would be like this, Sir, what a bloody war,
I'd like to go back home, Sir, don't want to fight no more.

The Quiet Trench Poet

Tommy met him in the trench,
Sitting quiet, writing, all alone,
Musing, maybe, of the fight just gone
or thinking of kinfolk safe at home;

"I've just returned from leave" he said,
"With special treats for all my mates,
But some of them are missing now,
Posted to a place with pearly gates";

I sat there silent, by his side,
Placed a hand of comfort on his arm,
He took the paper, with the words
that he had penned upon,
And placed them gently on my lap,
Suggesting I might read them later on;

I remembered, then, the words he wrote,
When I was told he'd said his last goodbye,
By being posted, 'missing',
Like many thousand soldiers gone before;

They were words of coming prophecy,
Telling how the world would be,
And told about the future,
When someone, close, remembered him in prayer,
And took the time to light a candle there ………

For Tommy and He

There is a candle for you Tommy, still,
And one for he, who would you kill,
Side by side they flicker, dignified and white;
From dawn's first glow till dark of night;

And when those candles melt to naught,
A hand appears, with candles brought,
And places them beside the melted tallow,
Where they will burn until a new tomorrow;

We will not forget you Tommy lad,
Nor the soldier who your life forbade,
You both now lay in Flanders clay,
Deprived of all your promised yesterdays;

Autumn comes, the leaves turn red and brown,
Wreaths for you and he are soft laid down,
As bugles sound goodbye, upon a given day,
For Tommy and that soldier dressed in grey.

(Ypres – 22 April 1915)

Gas Attack (1)

All quiet on the Western Front
mused acting Corporal Atkins,
All calm along the Allied lines,
Yet still the muddy salient groans,
In expectation of the battle to come,
In anticipation of a battle – hopefully to be won;
After many days of fighting
the human cargo of war
stumbled through the clay and rising water,
Setting sandbags higher still,
Trying hard to minimise the anticipated slaughter,
whilst shovels dug the final resting place
of soldiers now sacrificed,
Who would never have to face another day.
What the blinking hell is that?
Thought a puzzled Tommy Atkins,
As clouds of death progressed, ominously,
Creeping slowly across no man's land.
Thousands dying, thousands fleeing in panic,
Whilst the devil shouted more and more, encore.
The testing of chlorine gas had begun
along a confused and noisy Western Front.
The testing of Tommy's determination
once more, this time inside a respirator.

Trench Talk with Sgt Lucas

I don't hear no cheers, Sarge, when the gas clouds come our way,
Can you feel my fear, Sarge, I don't want to choke today;
I've tried to hide my tears, Sarge, listened hard to what you say,
I can take your jeers, Sarge, but make the gases go away.

Gas Attack (2)

"That fog's a funny colour Captain, looks a bit like custard"
"That's not fog you bloody fool, that's gas mixed up with mustard!"
All the soldiers present there put on their respirators,
But for one who sat alone, his trousers round his gaiters,
By the time he heard the shout of 'Gas' behind the breaker,
All his cheeks had blisters on and he had met his Maker;
This made his mates unhappy, when thinking later on,
About the tragic situation and the way their chum had gone.

Gas Instruction

So the Generals issued bulletins, to make the lads less glum,
Drop your trousers, if you must, but don't expose your bum,
Dress yourselves in underwear that has a buttoned flap,
Stand astride the wooden seat and aim between the gap;
Satisfied they said no more, for the soldiers clearly knew,
What it was that threatened them when sitting on the loo;
Now the Padres ain't involved in giving absolution
to the privates, caught at odds, performing their ablutions.

(The Somme – December 1915)

No Man's Land

The Moon of the Somme stared down,
At the bleak landscape in no man's land,
Barbed wire, hiding in drifts of windswept snow,
Held tight to the carcasses of death,
Slumped, as rag dolls, along their coiling lines,
And Satan laughed at the splendour of it all;
Sheets of white, folded like a crease
along the edges of the hand dug trenches,
Dripped water to the mud below, causing pools to form
around boots, filled with gelid toes, wrapped in soggy hose,
As the blankets slept with tired and weary men;

Frost settled deep on the bough of naked, ravaged, trees,
Asleep until the spring, and the wind blew devoid of pity;
Rats scurried from crater to crater,
Nibbling flesh from the frozen sacrifices,
Squeaking a 'thank you' to the Angel of Death,
Before departing to the safety of a shell hole,
Waiting for the night to grow
Into another day of watching and waiting;
And the wind sang the Song of Satan, cold and bitter;

The sky turned from black to reluctant grey,
Time marched, with hesitant step, through the waking lines,
As the winter Sun arrived in an apologetic haze,
From the cookhouse sparked a blaze of fire
stoked by silhouettes in greatcoats;

Bacon smells drifted on the early morning air,
Tempting the starved warriors from their foxholes;
Hot tea, poured into chipped enamel mugs,
Warmed the fingers of the lambs of slaughter,
The men who would ask no quarter
or yield to the thought of dying,
When the sting of bullet or bayonet thrust
Would send them sprawling in the solid dust;

Perhaps the Sun was empty,
Perhaps the gods forgot to care,
For there was nothing there,
To warm the hearts of stone, or thaw the misery;
The trenches were left alone, held in a grip of despair,
Listening, praying, for the sound of spring,
But hearing only the dull ache of an endless winter.

(The Somme – 30 June 1916)

A Soldier's Prayer

I am a soldier, about to die a soldier's death,
I suppose I should kneel and pray
about the present situation;
The air is still, the earth groans and moans
with mortal remains;
Upon the bloodied soil lies a carpet of bodies,
Within the trenches lies the General's folly,
Out there an isolated voice is crying like a baby,
Voices are screaming like tortured men;
I am a soldier, about to die a soldier's death,
But then again, perhaps not!

I am a soldier hoping to survive,
Maybe the 'zinging' bullet will miss me,
And the screaming shell pass me by?
Perhaps my khaki body will miss the sniper's eye,
And the 'rat tat tat' of spitting gun
will spew its leaden death,
Upon some other hapless soul, instead of me,
But then again, perhaps not!

German soldiers petition like me,
They talk to the same Christian Deity,
Or so I'm told!
They are no braver hearted,
No more cavalier, or bold;
Their fears call out loud or silent thinking;

I wonder if He thinks of them, or me?
As we wait to do our soldier duty;
Dreading the thought of sacrificial death,
As He who once 'died' upon a rugged tree,
But then again, perhaps not;

I am a soldier not wanting to die a soldier's death,
Rats watching me, lice scratching at my skin,
As I utter a meaningful Amen;
No bread, no jam, no tins of bully beef,
No tea at all;
Please God, if I am to die out there,
Please let me die like a soldier,
Don't let me die alone!

(The Somme – 1 July 1916)

Slaughter on the Somme

A sunlit sky promised a day of oppressive heat,
(In more ways than one)
The River Somme, silent and unwary
flowed lazily through the Allied lines,
Tommy Atkins checked his rifle once again;
It was six o'clock in the morning,
A dawn that would lend the day to distant mourning;

Three armies held their breath,
Soon, too soon, thousands would meet their death,
Long before that July day was done,
Long before this battle would be lost, or bloodied, won;

Five days after a heavy bombardment,
(That was supposed to clear the way)
Thought a hopeful Tommy Atkins;
The blast of whistle told the soldiers brave,
Time to clamber up the ladders to the top,
Walk casually across no man's land,
Like the Generals and the Colonels said we should;

'Over the top' they went, the many 'pals' Battalions,
Until the forward soldiers began to drop
into the shell holes, that would become their graves,
Soldiers falling dead, on the fallen dead;

Evening told the story of that sun-drenched fateful day,
What once was grass had turned to bloodied chalk and clay,
Soldiers slumped and dying in a captured German trench,
The British and the Germans and the French;
River Somme, now stained with fighting soldiers' blood,
Flowed slowly through the scattered Allied lines.

(Mid-July 1916)

Stories from the Trenches

I've heard stories in the trenches,
Told in soft and whispered tones,
How the soldiers from Newfoundland,
Walked by trenches filled with soldiers dead as stone,
Who only hours before had sat and cursed together,
As they waited for the whistle to be blown;

Over humps and holes the squaddies poured,
Treading purposely like those who went before,
Round craters made by cannon shells that roared,
Spitting deadly metal into bodies, chalk and soil;
Yet still they marched, determined,
(Whispered voices proud proclaimed)
Towards the German trenches in the valley down below;

There they met a hail of bullets,
That cut and turned their khaki bodies round,
But with arms composed across their heaving chests,
And heads pressed into shoulders, hunched but square,
They advanced defiant across the bloodied ground;

By midday the fight was over,
With khaki bodies lying slaughtered everywhere,
Over 700 missing, wounded, killed;
Sixty-eight corps men still standing, shouting 'Sir'
As the 'roll call' told a story of despair.

At 8:45 a.m. on 1 July 1916, the Newfoundland Regiment and 1st Battalion of the Essex Regiment, were situated at St. John's Road, a support trench 250 yards (230 m) behind the British forward line and out of sight of the enemy. They received orders to move forward. Movement forward through the communication trenches was not possible because they were congested with dead and wounded men and under shellfire. Lieutenant Colonel Arthur Lovell Hadow, the battalion commander, decided to move immediately into attack formation and advance. As they breasted the skyline behind the British first line, they were effectively the only troops moving on the battlefield and clearly visible to the German defenders. Subjected to the full force of the 119th (Reserve) Infantry Regiment, most of the Newfoundland Regiment who had started forward were dead, dying or wounded within fifteen to twenty minutes of leaving St. John's Road trench. Source: Wikipedia

(Mid-July 1916)

Quiet in my Dugout

I sit inside my muddy shelter, Cpl Thomas Atkins,
Singing words I one time heard upon a gramophone;
'When he fancies he is past love,
It is then he meets his first love,
For his first love is his last love,
And he loves her as he never loved before'
As I sleep and dream of fighting gone before,
The notes of song invite themselves into my image of this war;
'Did the dashing Dinks not win a battle?
In some dike for history,
Don't some soldiers now lie 'resting',
In some new dug cemetery?
In my dreams she runs her fingers through my dirty unkempt hair,
Wanting more I feel for comfort, but I find no comfort there;
Sleeping deep, with eyes half open,
Gazing sightless at a cold and cloudy sky,
Sleeping deep, with mouth wide open,
Twitching slightly as he dreams of yesterday's war.

(The Battle of Flers-Courcette – 15–22 September 1916)

Introducing the Tank

The Generals told the Colonels,
And the Colonels told the men,
About a brand new weapon,
They would be using now and then,
The tank, about to end the war of wars;

Tommy wondered what this weapon would be like,
But he thought it would be super, really great,
If it put the Hun to fleeing, what a sight!
This tank would end this long, long, war,
But where had we heard that statement before?

It came clanking down the roadway,
Squelching over soggy ground,
Until it stood defiant beside the intrigued men,
This tank that might end this protracted war;

When the fighting was all over,
And the tale of this new weapon did unfold,
That it wasn't quite as lethal as was told;
So the Colonels told the Generals what they knew,
And the Generals said 'Cor Blimey'
back to the drawing board.

The development of tanks in World War One was a response to the stalemate that trench warfare had created on the Western Front. Research took place in both Great Britain and France. The French fielded their first tanks in April 1917. The Germans, on the other hand, began development only in response to the appearance of Allied tanks on the battlefield. Whilst the Allies manufactured several thousand tanks during the war, Germany deployed only twenty of her own. Source: Wikipedia

(The Battle of Flers-Courcelette – 15–22 September 1916)

Shoulder to Shoulder

A dramatic dawn sky,
Presaged a hot summer day;
Steadfast eyes consulted firmly held timepieces,
It was five o'clock in the morning.
Tommy stood shoulder to shoulder
With his pals, geared up to go,
Expecting to close with the foe,
Waiting and hoping to strike the first blow;
Men, good and true, though none of them knew
who would survive that long day?
Stared with jaws square and steady,
Awaiting the time the kismet whistle blew;
Out of the trenches they climbed,
Extending from shoulder to shoulder,
Into a line that some pen would define
As a line of determined intention;
Over the soil, that no man's soil,
That would drink the blood of the brave;
But who would be counting the cost,
Counting the wounded, the dead and the lost,
Not the poet who captured, in quick lines, the sight,
But the Generals who started the fight.

A subsidiary attack of the Somme Offensive, the Battle of Flers-Courcelette was notable for the introduction of tanks. The attack was launched across a 12 km front from Rawlinson's Fourth Army salient on 15 September. Twelve divisions were employed, along with the forty-nine tanks the British Army possessed. Accordingly, on 11 September the forty-nine tanks began to move slowly into position in the line. As a measure of their fundamental unreliability, seventeen tanks were unable to make it as far as the front line. Of the twenty-two that did, a further seven failed to work at zero hour. Thus fifteen of the forty-nine tanks rolled slowly into no man's land with the start of the attack on 15 September. Source: firstworldwar.com

The cool of the evening descended at last,
With mist hanging low on the hill,
Soldiers, now spent, sitting quiet and still,
Thanked God for their prayed for deliverance;
Whilst out on the land, the land of no man
Death's stillness crept out to the fallen;
And chums, who no more would grow any older
or know of the price they had paid,
Lay silently, shoulder to shoulder,
Awaiting the cold of a shallow dug grave.

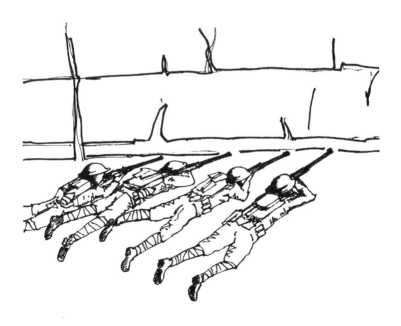

(Poperinge – Spring 1917)

Egg and Chips

We're standing down tomorrow,
Pass the word along the line,
We'll soon be off to R and R,
To leave this wretched war behind;
And we hope it will be Poperinge!
We can almost smell the
egg and chips from here;
Leave behind the trenches and the wire,
The killing and the sound of angry field gun fire,
The squalor and the smell of no man's land;
Thank God we're standing down tomorrow;

We'll be scrubbing down tomorrow,
In a town behind the line,
It may well be
Getting rid of lice and smelly underwear,
And feeling much the better, for a time;
There may be drill and weapon training,
It may be dry, it may be raining,
But we won't care a bit;
At dusk there'll be an end to it,
We're standing down tomorrow;

We'll be stepping out tomorrow, after dark,
Making for the centre of the town,
Heading for the cafes and drinking places,
Looking for a spot to settle down;
Ordering a beer and plate of something special,
That the waitress will be glad to bring our way,
As she walks towards our table,
With her lovely swaying hips,
Carrying our plates of egg and chips;
It's the treat we will look forward to, tomorrow.

Trench Talk with Sgt Wilson

Can I have a smoke, Sarge, would like to have a fag,
Tell another joke, Sarge, this war's a blinking drag,
Didn't know you were sleeping, Sarge, never saw your tunic sag,
Sorry that I spoke, Sarge, think I'll have another fag!

(Ypres – July 1917)

Heading for the Front Line

Horses pull your limbers up the 'grab and stumble' road,
Loaded up with food and timber, another heavy load;
Heading for the front line, heading for a bad time,
I wish the rain would cease;

Rain, Rain, go away, it's just another Sunday,
When the Padre's preaching why I should believe –
in God!

Mud, mud, glorious mud,
Nothing quite like it for mixing with blood,
So follow me, follow, down to the hollow,
And there let us wallow in somebody's blood;
Packed my big pack and my pouches,
Shaving soap and War Department issue 'housewife'!
Dragging on a 'Woodbine', heading for the front line
I just wish the rain would cease;

Rain, Rain, go away, it's just another 'one day'
When my mind is reaching for my folk back home!

Send another message on the 'Fuller' telephone,
Tell them we are coming and they are not alone,
In praying for some sunshine, heading for the front line,
I wish the rain would cease;

Rain, Rain, go away, it's just another Monday,
And the Sergeant's teaching how I can deceive –
the enemy!

Mud, mud, glorious mud,
Nothing quite like it, this Passchendaele mud,
So follow me, follow, down to the hollow,
And there let us wallow in British and German race blood;
Cleaned my kit and rifle, safely sheltered in my dugout,
Soaked, my boots and gaiters, 'what's this bloody war about?'
Dragging on a 'Woodbine', sitting on the front line,
I wish the rain would cease.

(Passchendaele – September 1917)

Tomorrow I Go over the Top

Ten o'clock at night, one more hour to go before I am relieved,
The chance to go back to my dugout and greasy cup of tea;
Then the routine of the last few weeks,
Two hours on, four hours off, 'stand to' at dawn and dusk, ends;
Tomorrow we all go over the top, our chance, at last,
To end the boredom and waiting;
Tomorrow I'm going over the top,
To kill me a German or two,
But that won't be anything new, tomorrow;

Looking down at my boots, wet and muddy,
(what would the Sergeant Major say?)
Glancing around at my roof of corrugated iron,
Walls of sandbags, chalk and timber;
Reflecting that this has been home, for the last few weeks;
Tomorrow I'm going over the top,
To wipe out a German or two,
Just one sleepless night to get through, before tomorrow;

Sleep refuses to calm my brain,
I start thinking of home, the smell of Mum's cooking,
The infectious laughter of my sister, Auntie Peg's hugs,
Ben's barking, and the comfort of my back room bed;
I wish I was going home tomorrow….. but tomorrow
I go over the top;

Hands steadier than I could have imagined,
Fag stuck defiant in dry cracked lips,
Smiling as Bert slides and slips in the mud –
trying to regain his balance and dignity;
The scramble will begin, up and over the top
watching for someone to stop,
The first bullet of defiance and resistance;
Somehow I know tomorrow will be my last day,
The day I climb out of this trench – for the last time;
Tomorrow we're going over the top,
To fight with a German or two,
The day that my living is through, tomorrow!

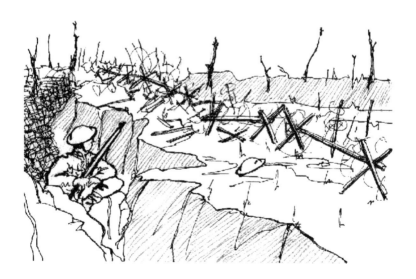

(Passchendaele – September 1917)

The Young Subaltern

Wetting his cracked lips with whisky,
He tried to keep his sarcasm under control,
But his mind had nowhere to go,
Except back to the trenches on the front,
Somewhere not far from the 'Salient' hump;
'It isn't the thought of dying', he considered,
'It's the fear of having to continue fighting –
until we are the chosen few,
Who will live to remember every day,
Whose memories will have many tricks to play';

Licking his lips, still wet with whisky,
He continued, 'It's going to get worse,
This sod of a war, this Passchendaele curse,
This desecration of the most evil kind,
Nothing matters to beast or mankind';

Recalling his orders, he continued to drink,
'Don't dare to complain, never try to explain,
Can't damp the spirits of the chaps, what!
Can't take away their enduring camaraderie;
Best not to look them straight in the eye,
Their friends are lying around them,
Slaughtered by this unspeakable shame,
It's all too unreal, so bloody insane'!

Junior officers, some as young as seventeen and mostly volunteers from public schools, suffered a casualty rate twice that of other ranks and their average life expectancy at the front was just six weeks. The universal expectation of a subaltern was "a hospital bed or interment in the soil". A seemingly insignificant shrapnel wound might result in death a fortnight later. Shell and mortar fragments were responsible for sixty per cent of infantry wounds and rifle and machine gun bullets thirty-five per cent. School magazines show an officer death rate from bullets at forty to fifty per cent. This was because the officers led their men into battle and made obvious and sensible targets for German troops. What saved this haemorrhaging of subalterns was a reorganisation of tactics. Source: *Daily Express* book review

(Passchendaele – September 1917)

Over the Top

When I dropped I knew I had copped a Blighty,
Or something worse! no time to sit and curse,
Blood told me I had been hit,
But strangely, I felt no pain, no discomfort;
Funny, I thought, of course no leg no pain;
But for the fear in my throat I would have laughed –
at the insaneness of my thinking;
Medic…. Medic…… Medic
I'm lying in this crater, please help me Bandage Joe;

God I'm cold, I'm frightened, no I'm scared –
maybe I'm dying, can't nobody see me?
Remember your first aid, remember what they said,
Give yourself a morphine jab,
Place a bandage over the wound,
What blinking wound? Pull the bandage tight,
Tight, tight, my hands can't grip,
Oh! To hell with it, Oh! To hell with me;
Why do I keep making these silly remarks? I expect it's the morphine;
Medic…. Medic…… Medic
I'm dying in this hellhole, please come Bandage Joe;

I felt the shrapnel, then I heard the shell
burst above my head, now I'm very dead,
Buried in this crater (too late Bandage Joe!),
Covered by this foreign soil,
That so many men would die for –
In the morning of their lives.

(11 November 1918)

Battle Song

'Sing a song of sixpence, a pocket full of rye,
Ten Valiant soldier boys marching off to die'

Ten world war fighting men in the mud and slime,
One died of dysentery, now there are nine;

Nine German soldier boys fearful of their fate,
One got his legs blown off, now there are eight;

Eight Russian soldier boys looking up to heaven,
One had his head blown off, now there are seven;

Seven Turkish soldier boys up to all their tricks,
One stepped on to a mine, now there are six;

Six Aussie soldier boys wanting badly to survive,
One was plain unlucky 'sport', now there are five;

Five 'Sepoy' soldier boys sick to death of war,
One ran off, they shot him dead, now there are four;

Four Austrian soldier boys home on wounded leave,
One died in hospital, now there are three;

Three 'Taffy' soldier boys never really knew,
What it was that clouted them, now there are two;

Two Flanders soldier boys, one a father one a son,
Fired at each other, now there's only one;

One lonely soldier boy, with no one left to slay,
Took his steel rimmed helmet off and threw his gun away;

'Then the war was over, what a thankful thing,
Wasn't that a great despatch to send home to the king?'

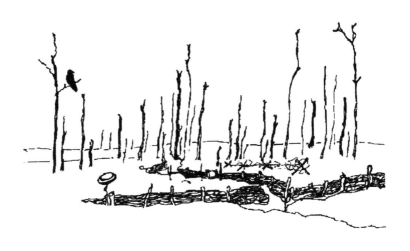

The Queue

Since I joined the army all I seemed to do is queue,
Queue for 'jabs' and "Cough twice please",
Queue for guns at the armoury,
Even queued to have a bath,
Thank God there is no queue to laugh!

'Still in this queue,
So many men in front of me,
Behind me stand so many more,
Forming an endless queue'

I have queued to have my hair cut short,
Queued for my pay and leave pass,
Queued for a pint in a NAAFI glass,
Often queued to use the loo,
Thank God that was always a shorter queue!

'Lots of silence in this queue,
Single file, not two by two,
Slowly forward, rest, then on again;
Thought I heard a choir's refrain?'

Queued to reach an active trench,
Queued to join the battered French,
Loads of mud on boots and gaiters,
No queue it seems to reach that crater;
'But I could not reach it, why oh!, why?

'Almost to the gate now,
Nobody left in front of me,
What a day to die!
Good morning St. Peter'.

Telegram Boy

A youth, not much younger than the soldier,
Named within the black edged telegram he held,
Turned his red painted bicycle into the head of the road,
A road that led towards the address of that young soldier,
Cpl Tommy Atkins;
A curtain, held in a trembling hand, twitched,
A relieved voice whispered, "Thank you God",
as the telegram boy rode by, searching for number thirty-three,
Looking for a foretold black and yellow painted door;
He whistled softly, and the privet hedge rustled
as he placed his bike against it, and opened the front gate;
He made his way respectfully to the front door,
Behind which stood the waiting mum of
Cpl Thomas Atkins;
Trembling fingers turned the mortise key,
As thumping veins beat inside her anxious head,
This was the moment her aching heart had dreaded;
Watery eyes read the short unwanted message,
"Missing in action, presumed dead",
"Thank you, son", she whispered to the lad,
Who turned, and walked back to his waiting bicycle;
For a moment, she thought,
He looked just like her son,
But he wasn't her son!
Her son is, now, officially dead.

World War One brought a large increase in telegraph traffic. During 1915, ninety-one million messages were handled in the United Kingdom. The delivery boys and girls cycled very fast to the address on the envelope and waited in case the person getting the message wanted to reply. Sometimes, the envelope had a special mark and the delivery boy or girl knew not to wait because it was bad news and there would be no reply. During the war, people were very nervous when a telegram arrived. When a soldier in the army had been wounded, was missing or had been killed, his family got the news in a telegram. Source: Schools WW1

Why My Son?

I can hear the crowds outside,

Cheering, clapping and singing;

Four years ago I had stood with them,

Cheering and shouting goodbye to my son;

I suppose the crowds outside,

Cheering, clapping and singing,

Are pleased that the war is over,

Glad that we have won;

I can understand all that clapping and cheering,

But my heart aches, for my lost son.

Part Two

Beyond the Menin Gate

Part of the speech of Lord Plumer of Messines at the unveiling of the Menin Gate, Ypres, 1927

One of the most tragic features of the Great War was the number of casualties reported as missing believed killed. When peace came, and the last ray of hope had been extinguished, the void seemed deeper and the outlook more forlorn for those who had no grave to visit, no place where they could lay tokens of loving remembrance...

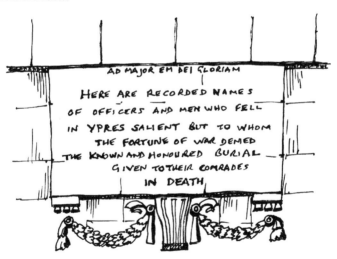

.......and it was resolved that here at Ypres, where so many of the missing are known to have fallen, there should be erected a memorial worthy of them which should give expression to the nation's gratitude for their sacrifice and their sympathy with those who mourned them. A memorial has been erected which, in its simple grandeur, fulfils this objective, and now it can be said of each one, in whose honour we are assembled here today:
"He is not missing; he is here!"

The Ghosts Beneath the Menin Gate

'Who will buy my bright red poppies,
Perhaps there's someone willing?'

Where is this place I find myself? I rise to mount my steed,
My breastplate in the sun reflects the glory of my deeds;
What is this sound that calls me here? Four bugles in accord,
I ride beneath the Menin Gate, my graveyard, my reward;
This arch becomes Jerusalem to all the men who fell,
This arch is close to Passchendaele, I know this place so well;
Rise up men, go rise up then, depart this place once seen;
Rise up men, rise up again, the fields have turned to green.

Trumpets sound the battle cry, the knights, once more, respond,
Their helmets in the sun reflect the glory from beyond;
Behind them stand the battlements, where once they stood to fight,
Before them stretch the open fields, filled with gravestones, white,
They feel the firmness of the ground, the tanks they now have gone,
Memories are all that's left; the guns no more belong;
Rise up men, go rise up then, come hear the 'last post' call,
Rise up men; rise up again, that sound will touch us all.

'Who will buy my bright red poppies,
Each one worth at least a shilling!

(Words and Sounds of Brass 1)

The Sound of Brass

Dead eyed he slumped, no more to speak,
No more to curse the 'big gun' sounds,
Like so many other soldier boys had done;

No more to swear, no throat to clear of phlegm,
No more to hear the Padre's hastened mumble of farewell,
Death had visited, borne high on field gun rumble;

Peace, conclusively found, he has no head to crown,
No ear to cup, no eye to close in sleep or sadness,
Slowly his body will succumb to nameless worm.

-0-0-0-0-0-0-0-0-

Closed tight the curtains, large tears fall softly,
Whispered goodbyes drift from the English shires;
So sits alone the widow,
So lies alone the sacrificed;

-0-0-0-0-0-0-0-0-

Shall life, anew, creep from his fractured frame,
Shall words, on paper, succour to his loved ones give,
Shall his sacrifice be venerated in the future years?

The sounds of brass have blown a sad farewell,
For truth to tell the warrior came to fight,
But found, instead, the meaning of true hell,
Within the trenches, mire, and dead men's blood.

(Words and Sounds of Brass 2)

Any Words Now Said

Name are chiselled here, names once flesh and bone,
Accompanied by sounds that ring from Heaven's throne;
Yet war, and sacrifice, are words that I deplore,
No pardon can be issued from these monuments of stone;

No sad reflection, now, can alter history,
Contrition finds no place in all that misery,
Too many words have slain the brave before,
There are no offerings that speak for tragedy;

No words can heal the wounds from battles fought,
Broken bodies, dead, contain no thought;
Yet cries of men still issue from that gore,
The gore that shell and shrapnel burst have brought;

I often feel that never flows more red,
The blood that man, and war, so oft have bled;
Where bodies, wasted by the greed of war,
Can never be replaced by any words now said.

A Tommy Dies

In his youth he had joined in the battles,
With his cousins, their fathers, their brothers,
Not wanting to die, but seeing men die,
Without a word of complaint,
And often without a whispered goodbye;
The ears of that time heard the trench men's songs,
Songs that had real meaning;
The ears of that time heard the screaming
Of far ranged bullet or shell,
Turning his trench into images of mud and blood,
Until peace rescued him and he was sent back home.

In the calm of the evening of his life,
He would walk down country lanes
Admiring the spring lacework of cow parsley,
Feeling his elderly aches and pains;
The hoot of an owl resonating sweet in his ear,
The sound of the cuckoo sounding distant but clear,
Sounds of concord, sounds of cheer.

In the midst of a night he would die,
Weathered skin resting on worn out veins,
Veins stagnate on matured brittle bones;
No night bird singing a melody sweet,
No clarion call to send him on his way,
His past sealed, forever, in the stillness of his heart;
A heart no longer beating, finally retreating,
From the whimpers and groans
Of that conflict long ago.

(Westminster Abbey – 1920)

The Unknown Warrior

I did not see the twenties

Or the journey to my grave;

The thirties or the forties

For I lie within the nave,

In an Abbey for the 'famous'

Described as 'The Unknown';

All I hear is congregations

And their hymns sung choral clear,

Around me stand my people

With their thoughts of one so dear,

Their friend, their son, their father

Or the lover they had known;

For it is only I that knows me

Yet I can't speak my name,

Is that fame or just misfortune?

Perhaps they are the same;

My face is but a mystery,

Unknown and yet well known.

The British Tomb of the Unknown Warrior holds an unidentified British soldier killed on a European battlefield during the First World War. He was buried in Westminster Abbey, London on 11 November 1920, simultaneously with a similar interment of a French unknown soldier at the Arc de Triomphe in France, making both tombs the first to honour the unknown dead of the First World War. It is the first example of a Tomb of the Unknown Warrior. Source: Wikipedia

'Epilogue'

What will they think of us,
A hundred years from now,
The people yet unborn?
Will they lift their faces to the sky,
Will they feel the need to cry,
For their fathers, who had died,
On those battlefields of Flanders;
'Blow your bugle, soldier ghost,
To the waiting angel hosts,
Play your anthem and last post;

What will they learn from us,
A thousand years from now,
The daughters yet unborn?
Will they feel the need to breed,
Will they watch their children bleed,
For some undetermined creed,
On the craters of Selene?

What will they make of us,
Ten thousand years from now,
The sons who know it all?
Will they say we died in vain,
And deride our bloody shame,
Then do it all again –
and again, again, again……